This is dedicated to Aaliyah, Tiana, Thomas, Cookie and Dennis ♡

Copyright © 2020 by Tiny Angel Press LTD.

All rights reserved.

No part of this book may be reproduced, stored in a retrieval system, or transmitted in any form or by any means, electronic, mechanical, photocopying, recording, scanning, or otherwise, without the prior written permission of the publisher.

https://themonster-series.com

Illustrations by Dmitry Chizhov

Thanks to author Karen McMillan for her assistance with this project.

ISBN: 978-1-9163503-7-3

In collaboration with Duckling Publishing and Chrissy Metge Ltd.
www.ducklingpublishing.com
www.chrissymetge.com

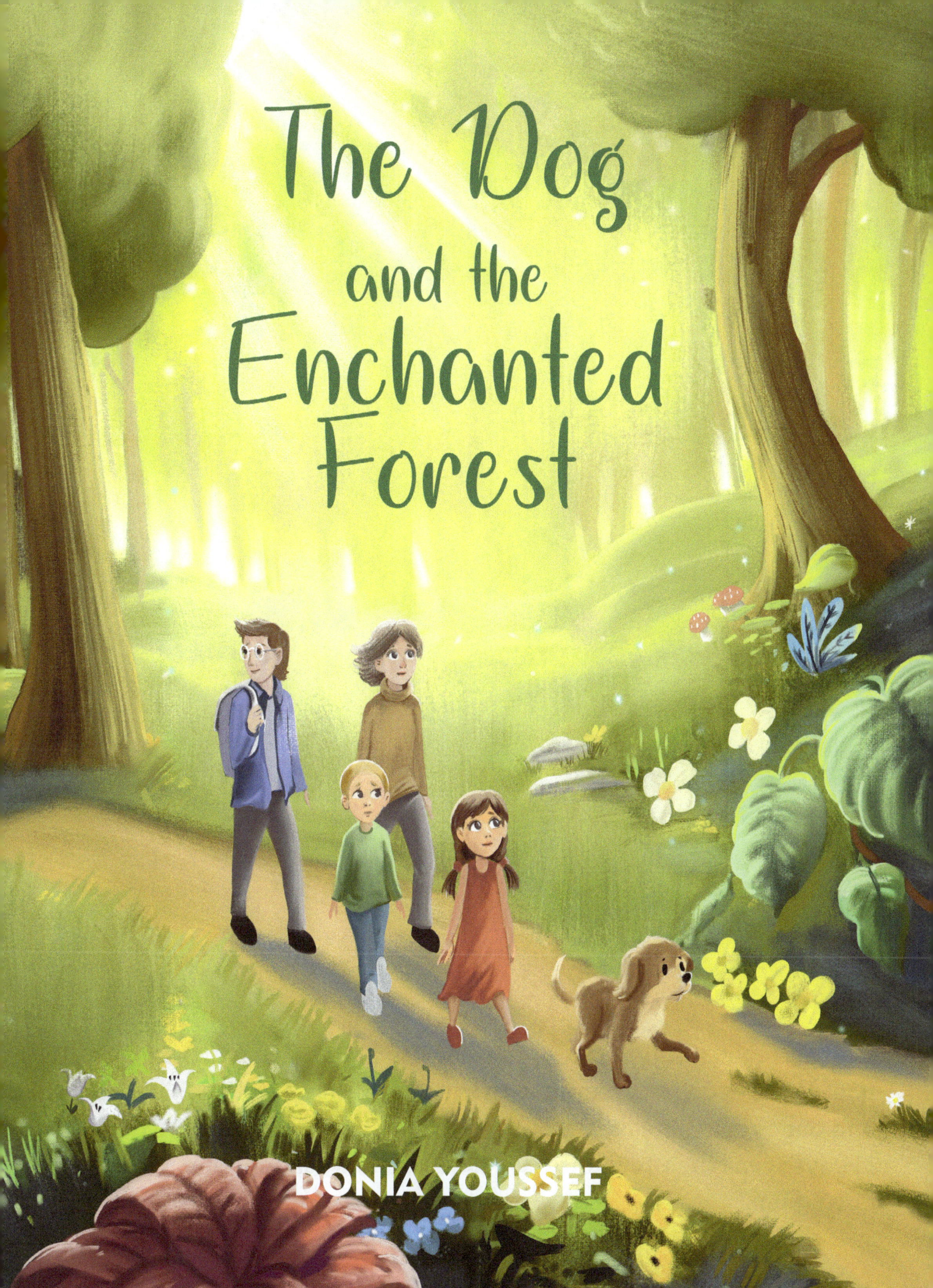

It was a regular autumn Saturday morning in Jasmine and Brianna's house. The little girls played with their toys on the floor, while Mummy and Daddy made breakfast. Every weekend was the same. The family always spent their favourite two days of the week together, playing and having fun.

Suddenly, there came a faint sound from outside. Jasmine and Brianna slowly and quietly went towards the door. It sounded like something weakly clawing and scratching. The two little sisters put their ears against the wood and heard a soft whimpering

'Mum, Dad, there's someone here,' Jasmine whispered.

'Wait... Get back.' Dad quickly came and the sisters stood behind him.

Dad opened the door and looked around. 'There's no one there.' Dad said.

'Dad! Look down. It's a little puppy.' Jasmine and Brianna went to inspect it closely.

'He's shaking!' Jasmine said.

'He doesn't look well. Can we bring him in?' Brianna asked, and Mum and Dad nodded.

Jasmine picked the little dog up and set him down in front of the fire. The dog looked restless. He stood in front of the fire for a few seconds, but then started walking towards the door. Whenever the sisters would try to bring him back, he gave them a whimper and a gentle bark.

'Why won't he sit? He should warm up.' Brianna was confused.

'Maybe he's hot,' Jasmine said and carried the dog to the couch, away from the fire. But the same thing happened again.

'Let him go, girls. Let's see what he does,' Mum said, and they all watched intently.

The dog went to the door and started scratching it.

'He wanted to get inside, and now he wants to go out?' Jasmine was confused.

'Maybe he wants to tell us something,' Dad said, and they all went towards the door.

Brianna opened the door and the dog started running along the path. But when he turned around and saw that the family wasn't following him, he walked a few steps back and barked at them.

'He wants us to follow him!' Brianna exclaimed and went out with her sister.

'Not so fast, girls. Let's get our coats and something to eat for the road first,' Mum said and went to the kitchen to get a healthy snack. 'Some fruit will do just fine.'

Then Mum caught up to the rest of the family. The tiny dog walked and walked without stopping. He looked so tired but didn't give up. Jasmine and Brianna were getting tired too, but they could sense that their mission was an important one. Seeing the dog walking doggedly through the forest, the family wouldn't stop for anything.

Suddenly, the forest around them started to change. As they went deeper and deeper, it got lighter and lighter. Everything around became more colourful and beautiful. The trees were greener and the flowers more vibrant.

'Let's hurry; it's a little farther,' the dog said.

'Wait! You can talk?' Jasmine exclaimed.

'Only in the Enchanted Forest,' the dog said, and they were so amazed, they followed him without saying a word.

After a while, the family came to a river and saw all kinds of animals, lying on the ground, gasping for air.

'What happened here?' the sisters wondered and went around to see if they could help the animals.

'I don't know,' the dog said. 'They're all sick.'

'Why aren't you sick?' asked Jasmine.

'I don't know that either. I woke up late today. When I came to the river to drink some water, I saw the other animals lying on the ground.'

'It's curious how they're all here. Not scattered around the forest. Just here, near the river,' said Brianna.

'The river!' Jasmine exclaimed. 'That must be it!'

'Yes! It has to be the river,' Brianna agreed.

Carefully, trying not to touch the water, Brianna leaned over and inspected it closely.

'It is a greenish colour and smells funny. The problem is definitely the water,' Brianna declared.

'We have to do something. Otherwise, other animals might drink and get sick,' said Jasmine.

'You go, girls,' said Mum. 'We'll stay here and try to help the sick animals.'

'I didn't drink the water. I'll help you,' a bird said, flying into the sky.

Mum and Dad went around the forest and gathered the best flowers, healthy herbs, fruits and vegetables. They got all the animals to eat something and cleaned them up as well as they could. In the meantime, Jasmine and Brianna had the toughest task of their lives before them. They ran beside the river, trying to find what was poisoning the water. The bird followed them from up above and kept and eye out as well.

Suddenly, the sisters saw something suspicious. A big pipe was cracked and leaking green, gooey and smelly liquid into the river.

'There! There's the leak!' Jasmine exclaimed.

'Okay, we'll need to plug it and make sure it never leaks again,' Brianna said.

'Birds are excellent builders. We can help you,' the bird said from the sky.

The bird cheeped and after just a minute, hundreds of birds appeared in the sky. During that time, the sisters gathered all the things that might help. They found a stone that fitted perfectly and carefully placed it in the cracked pipe.

'Oh, no, it's still leaking from the sides!' Jasmine said.

'Look!' Brianna pointed to the sky as the birds flew down towards the pipe.

One by one, the birds placed mixture they used to build their nests and filled up the hole.

'It's done!' Brianna exclaimed. 'It's not leaking anymore.'

'Will this hold?' Jasmine asked.

'We do this for a living, trust me, it will hold.' The birds were so happy they could help.

The girls ran back to spread the good news. When they reached the clearing where the animals had been lying around sick, they saw that all of them were up on their feet.

'We did it!' Jasmine said. 'The water is now safe to drink.'

'Us too!' Dad was excited. 'The animals are getting better.'

Word quickly spread and everyone heard of what the family did. The animals gathered around and thanked the sisters and their parents. They couldn't be happier. The family got ready to go back home and the animals made them promise to visit again. Jasmine and Brianna loved their first time in the Enchanted Forest, and they couldn't wait for the next adventure.

The Dog and the Enchanted Forest is one of several books I have written about the reality of facing cancer, and in this case, it is the danger of toxins on the health of those around us - both humans and animals.

After I released my first book *The Monster in Mummy*, I became more and more involved with different charities and organisations. Other cancer survivors then started to contact me and telling me their own stories. I realised there is so much we as a society are not aware of especially when it comes to what cancer survivors go through. Their stories are so powerful and yet we hardly heard from patients. Why is that? I am so humble and proud to be able to bring you these stories and help raise awareness that behind every cancer diagnostic is a real person.

Donia Youssef, Author & Producer of *The Monster series*.

www.ingramcontent.com/pod-product-compliance
Lightning Source LLC
Chambersburg PA
CBHW060503240426

43661CB00006B/897